Challenge Your Mind!
Write Creatively. I Did!

The Creative Writings of

Avionne L. Steele

Copyright © 2018

All rights reserved. Except for the inclusion of brief quotations in a review, no part of this book may be reproduced in any form without permission in writing from the author or publisher.

First Printing

ISBN 978-1-57550-076-8

Printed in the United States of America
May 2018

The stories and poems in this volume are all works of fiction. The characters and events portrayed are fictional and any resemblance to real people and incidents is pure coincidental.

INDEX

1 - Acrostic Poem - Avionne

2 - The Laughing Good Bird Named Blue

3 - The Adventures of Old Fixalot

8 - My Magic Box

9 - How to Make a Poem Explode

11 - The Tree of Sadness

13 - Variations on a Theme

14 - Variations on a Theme

15 - The Mysterious Kleiger Case

17 - The Kleiger Case Returns
     After 15 Long Years

Avionne La'Fay Steele

Acrostic Poem - Avionne

Awesome

Vivacious

Intelligent

Outstanding

New ideas

Nice

Easy-going

5th Grade, Luella Elementary School

Avionne La'Fay Steele

The Laughing Good Bird Named Blue

There once was a good bird named Blue.
Who loved to laugh and roll in a shoe.
Why doesn't he fly?
And touch the blue sky.
You could touch it too if you were Blue.

5th Grade, Luella Elementary School

Avionne La'Fay Steele

The Adventures of Old Fixalot

It was a rainy day and a little girl named Wonder from the town of Aqua, Georgia stood in amazement to see a snoring toddler fast asleep inside a pipe. She pulled the toddler out slowly and gently like one would pull out a Jenga block. She placed him on the pipe and said in a whisper, "How strange, I found a little kid in a pipe. You never see that around here. Anyway I must tell my mom!"

She woke him up and started pushing him along. Then she stopped. "Before we go in you have to meet T.K.F.P.C.," she said.

He looked at her and said, "The what?"

She stood up strong and said, "The Kids Fix Pipes Club, we fix pipes everywhere. So, until you are sixteen you'11 be living here with the members. You'll learn how to swim fast, understand any creature, you will hear greatly, and you'11 be able to fix anything!"

One day the boy met a pouting cricket with eyes as big as quarters. He said, "Hi cricket, would you like to be my sidekick?"

The cricket leaped for joy. The boy's afro looked like it was exploding from his head. The cricket jumped into the afro and made his home there.

Twelve years later, the boy was skilled and could do all the things that Wonder said that he would do. When he turned sixteen, Wonder cried for joy, but she was going to miss him like a baby misses its pacifier. Before he left, she gave him a lucky fork. He took the fork and stuck it in his hair.

When he left the kids club, he jumped high and touched the sky. Even the cricket was dancing in his hair. He graduated, and he was now free. He felt so happy that he could cry, but he pulled himself together. He went to buy blue overalls. When he came out of the store with his overalls, he started looking for a plumbing job. All he kept hearing was: "No, No, No, No, No, No, No, No, No!"

He was about to give up, but he saw the last and only HELP WANTED sign. The job didn't look as good as the other jobs, but it was better than nothing, he thought. He opened the creaky door and the entire door fell off. He took out his lucky fork and fixed it up in a snap. When the boss came, the man quickly handed the fork to the cricket and said, "Jimmy". He just then named the cricket, Jimmy.

Jimmy the cricket jumped quickly to get the fork and quickly back.

"Can I help you?", the boss said.

The boy looked and said, "Yes, I would like a job."

He smiled and said, "Then you are hired. Go and fix these sixty-eight houses with broken pipes, and then you can get your money."

The man ran as fast as he could. Five seconds

later the man was standing outside the boss' office.
"I'm done," the man said.
The boss was thrilled and amazed. He smiled and said happily, "Well, Old Fixalot is your new nickname! Here is your money. Come back tomorrow."
Every day, Old Fi.xalot came back to the boss' office, until Old Fixalot got a note ...
The note said:

Dear Old Fixalot,

I have to go to a meeting in Atlanta tomorrow. I was hoping that you would be able to watch over T.K.F.P.C. for me.

Thanks,
Wonder

Old Fixalot thought that this was a great honor. He told Jimmy the cricket to meet him at T.K.F.P.C. lab at 5:00A.M. The cricket ran as fast as a lightning bolt to the lab and waited for Old Fixalot by the door.
"I knew this would happen. Old Fixalot didn't teach me how to open the door," Jimmy the cricket said frustrated.

When Old Fixalot got there, he opened up the door and Wonder was running out of the door so fast that the wind behind her made the cricket fly from Fixalot's afro.

She shouted, "I am too late to talk about it right now'.' She ran to the train and arrived just in time. Wonder breathed a sigh of relief and boarded the train. Three miles later, the train was coming to an unsteady bridge over a lake. "Can twenty-nine thousand people make it over this bridge?" the train conductor thought.

When the train traveled over the bridge, the bridge started swaying like a hammock between two trees. Then the train started swaying too. The passengers started screaming. Then ... Boom! Everybody was drowning.

Old Fixalot was asleep in Aqua, Georgia. His keen ears heard the people screaming. So, Old Fixalot ran as fast as he could and made it to the train in thirty minutes.

Old Fixalot quickly jumped into the water. He saved the people one by one and Jimmy gave them mouth to mouth resuscitation and finally fainted. It was a very serious moment when Old Fixalot realized that he did not save everybody. When he looked under the water he saw one person that he was unable to save. Wonder was lying there, still as a rock. He swam to get her with a tear in his eye.

"Wonder, please speak to me!" Old Fixalot

said.

    Wonder just squinted and said, "Old Fixalot, you did good. Run the club for me and I'll be watching." Then her eyes closed. Wonder was as dead as a doorknob.

    Old Fixalot went to the surface and began crying a waterfall. He cried out, "NOOOOO! This cannot happen to me! I am only sixteen."

    As the days went by, Old Fixalot dedicated all the heroic things he did to his friend Wonder. He wanted to keep her memory alive.

    When Old Fixalot was confused or sad, he would look up to the sky and talk to Wonder. He thanked her for taking care of him, encouraging him, and teaching him.

    Every once in a while, he would swear that he could hear Wonder answering back, saying "You're welcome, Old Fixalot."

Avionne La'Fay Steele

My Magic Box

Anything can fit in my magic box including:

A howling bag of bones,

Monarchy monkeys,

Lucky dirt,

Droplets of clattering and splattering rain,

My overflowing dignity

A melon of Happiness and juicy goodness,

And the crackling whisper of the clouds

6th Grade, Luella Middle School

How to Make a Poem Explode

Listen up readers!

You're reading this the wrong way.

Stop doing what you're doing and
listen to what I say!

You're being too gentle with these words

Take charge!

Own them!

Breathe them!

Understand them!

Or you will be stranded and all alone.

Pick up that majestic pencil and

Write like you know what you're doing!

Write like your life depends on it!

Avionne La'Fay Steele

(because it does)

Free the words, let them fly!

They have no limits, not even the sky!

Teach your words the way they should go

Just shake, shake, shake them

And make them explode all day!

Don't just sit and write, use all of your might

And when you feel giddy

You'll know you did right!

So blow up those words all day and all night!

6th Grade, Luella Middle School

The Tree of Sadness

The soul was gone,
The sky was no longer blue.
The tree
Well,
The tree was dead.
Dead of sorrow
Dead of pain
Dead of misery
Dead of rain,
No one could save this tree,
He couldn't take anymore
He tried and tried,
But the tree said, "No more."
When the sun came,
the tree would hide,
When the wind came
the tree would cry,
Everything was gone,
And will no longer show,
The hero lost the battle,
And will no longer grow.
It was over,
No buts,
No untils,
No maybes,
Nothing would EVER happen!

Avionne La'Fay Steele

Everything felt weird!
It was over,
It's too late,
No more generations,
No more cares,
No more happy dreams,
It was time for a greater plan,
And I saw,
Because it came to be the melody,
I can't explain,
And I definitely can't describe it,
But sadly, I know I took too long,
So it did it his way,
So please my fellow tree,
Don't wait!
Don't hesitate!
Just Believe,
Tomorrow is not promised,
And it will never be,
Don't be this tree,
Please,
Don't

To: Tree of Sadness
From: Unknown

7th Grade, Luella Middle School

Avionne La'Fay Steele

Variations on a Theme

This is just to say
I have picked
the ripest,
juiciest peach
from your farm.

And which you
were probably
saving to make
sweet cobbler.

Forgive me.
It was
so flavorful,
and so tasty.

7th Grade, Luella Middle School

Variations on a Theme

This is just to say
I let the dog
In the house last night
and he broke the lamp,

which you were
probably using
for your book club.

Forgive me.
He looked so sad,
And so miserable.

7th Grade, Luella Middle School

The Mysterious Kleiger Case

On December 15, 1999 the Kleiger Family went to the Graystone Mountain for a once in a lifetime family get away. Cleo, the sixteen year old daughter, reportedly "hormonal and suicidal" according to her parents, personally asked her best friend, Josh Erikson, to help them get to the top of the mountain since he was a Mountain Ranger.

On December 16 at 10:00 A.M., Josh led the family of four to the top of the mountain. Josh reportedly showed them to a cabin where they would stay for the night, told them to unpack their bags, and then asked them to meet him in the *Crest of the Core* which was a type of town-square for the Graystone Mountain Park.

An hour later, the Kleiger Family waited at the *Crest of the Core* for Josh, but he never arrived.

On the way back to their cabin, they found a cold and traumatized Josh Erikson. He was found giggling but not blinking. Between the giggling his words were, "She is Comin', Comin'."

According to witnesses, he continued to repeat this phrase in between giggles. Cleo called H.Q. of the Mountain Rangers and reported the finding of Josh Erikson.

According to Cleo, the answer from H.Q. was not what she had expected. Instead of sending people to help, she was told to go to a nearby lagoon to save Josh. Cleo quickly got into a boat and was seen heading toward the center of the nearby lagoon. After that, she was reported missing.

According to police, no one has seen her after that mysterious night. Sadly, after three years of trying to figure out what happened to Cleo Kleiger, the case remains unsolved. Josh Erikson is currently in a mental hospital until the police and FBI have more answers.

Until further notice, the case shall be closed and will be classified as suicide.

Luella Middle School

Avionne La'Fay Steele

The Kleiger Case Returns After 15 Long Years

Years after the tragic disappearance Cleo Kleiger, the case has suddenly reopened. A man named Tim Tock reports that while he was walking up Graystone Mountain, he violently fell through what he believed was a "soft spot" of the mountain.

However, this "soft spot" turned out to be the entrance, which led to a secret door. When the authorities opened the door, one policeman reported, "There was blood dripping from the walls, the ceilings, everywhere!"

But that's not all the police saw. In fact, the policeman states, "There were words written in the blood!

One of the words was "two." Another word was "curse," and the main word was "Bex." The word that seemed to intrigue the authorities most was "Bex," because Bex was the little brother of Cleo Kleiger!

Was Bex behind it all? The police believed it was a strong possibility. This possibility was strengthened even more after after Leslie Fontain, a psychic of sorts, investigated the scene.

When Leslie read over the case and visited this hidden room, she explained that she could see the dead Cleo Kleiger. "The room was dripping in sappy blood," she told reporters, "Cleo Kleiger was in the back of the room, crying."

Leslie later told reporters and police that she believed the death of Cleo wasn't suicide, but rather murder. She also admitted that she believed that Bex was involved.

Police believed at first that perhaps Mrs. Fontain had a screw loose, that is until they confronted Cleo Kleiger's parents.

The authorities asked her mother what type of relationship Cleo and Bex had. The answer was shocking.

"Bex and Cleo used to love each very much ... until something happened," her mother told reporters and police.

"Bex and Cleo were attending a camp. At camp it was Fun Friday. Fun Friday," she explained, "was where the kids would do different activities outside, and who ever won these activities got a trophy.

So obviously, Bex and Cleo were the final two competing for the trophy, and both of my children struggled with sore losing. The final activity was a race, and when it started, Cleo took off while Bex was struggling so, so bad.

Finally, when they got close to the finish line, they were neck and neck. Reality came over Bex and I guess he knew he wasn't going to win so he got on top of his sisters back and made her fall! Cleo was angry after that and when she got second, oh ... she was so *mad*. She wasn't even thinking straight. She went up to him and punched him right in his eye.

But do you think my son would tolerate that? Nope. So they started fighting. Everyone tried to break it up, but they couldn't ... it got out of hand. I don't know how, but Cleo got a hold of a ... gun and she shot him two times. One in the foot and the other in the arm. That was the only time she called Bex his real name: Beckett."

After this was reported to police, everything started to connect. Leslie could see the ghost of Cleo Kleiger crying because Leslie believed that Cleo was feeling guilty for what she had done.

After figuring all of this out, the FBI thought it would be helpful to take a visit down to the Lagoon.

After searching the lagoon, they found a gun and chains at the bottom of the lake. They later dusted the gun for finger prints and found the gun was covered with Bex's finger prints. But what about the chains? "We believe that Bex wanted her to suffer," the police reported, "so he shot her and drowned her."

After gathering so much information, the FBI believe Cleo wrote the words on the wall in the secret shelter. They believe she wrote "two" because she shot Bex two times. They also believe "curse" and "Bex" meant she either wanted to get Bex back or Bex wanted to get her back. The weird thing about the case being open now is that Bex has gone missing. So the real question remains, where is Bex?

Luella Middle School

About the Author

Avionne is now an 8th grader, but has been inspired to write since she was in elementary school. Her desire is to inspire other children to use their God given talents and the world of imagination to write creatively and pursue their dreams.